OUR DOMESTIC RELATIONS:

Or, How to Treat the Rebel States.

BY HON. CHARLES SUMNER.

AT this moment our Domestic Relations all hinge upon one question: *How to treat the Rebel States?* No patriot citizen doubts the triumph of our arms in the suppression of the Rebellion. Early or late, this triumph is inevitable. It may be by a sudden collapse of the bloody imposture, or it may be by a slower and more gradual surrender. For ourselves, we are prepared for either alternative, and shall not be disappointed, if we are constrained to wait yet a little longer. But when the day of triumph comes, political duties will take the place of military. The victory won by our soldiers must be assured by wise counsels, so that its hard-earned fruits may not be lost.

The relations of the States to the National Government must be carefully considered, — not too boldly, not too timidly, — in order to see in what way, or by what process, *the transition from Rebel forms may be most surely accomplished.* If I do not greatly err, it will be found that the powers of Congress, which have thus far been so effective in raising armies and in supplying moneys, will be important, if not essential, in fixing the conditions of perpetual peace. But there is one point on which there can be no question. The dogma and delusion of State Rights, which did so much for the Rebellion, must not be allowed to neutralize all that our arms have gained.

Already, in a remarkable instance, the President has treated the pretension of State Rights with proper indifference. Quietly and without much discussion, he has constituted military governments in the Rebel States, with governors nominated by himself, — all of which testifies against the old pretension. Strange will it be, if this extraordinary power, amply conceded to the President, is denied to Congress. Practically the whole question with which I began is opened here. Therefore to this aspect of it I ask your first attention.

CONGRESSIONAL GOVERNMENT *vs.* MILITARY GOVERNMENT.

FOUR military governors have been already appointed: one for Tennessee, one for South Carolina, one for North Carolina, and the other for Louisiana. So far as is known, the appointment of each was by a simple letter from the Secretary of War. But if this can be done in four States, where is the limit? It may be done in every Rebel State, and if not in every other State of the Union, it will be simply because the existence of a valid State government excludes the exercise of this extraordinary power. But assuming, that, as our arms prevail, it will be done in every Rebel State, we shall then have *eleven* military governors, all deriving their authority from one source, ruling a population amounting to upwards of nine millions. And this imperatorial dominion, indefinite in extent, will also be indefinite in duration; for if, under the Constitution and laws, it be proper to constitute such governors, it is clear that they may be continued without regard to time, — for years, if you please, as well as for weeks, — and the whole region which they are called to sway will be a military empire, with all powers, executive, legislative, and even judicial, derived from one man in Washington. Talk of the "one-man power." Here it is with a vengeance. Talk of military rule. Here it is, in the name of a republic.

The bare statement of this case may put us on our guard. We may well hesitate to organize a single State under a military government, when we see where such a step will lead. If you approve one, you must approve all, and the National Government may crystallize into a military despotism.

In appointing military governors of States, we follow an approved example in certain cases beyond the jurisdiction of our Constitution, as in California and Mexico after their conquest and before peace. It is evident that in these cases there was no constraint from the Constitution, and we were perfectly free to act according to the assumed exigency. It may be proper to set up military governors for a conquered country beyond our civil jurisdiction, and yet it may be questionable if we should undertake to set up such governors in States which we all claim to be within our civil jurisdiction. At all events, the two cases are different, so that it is not easy to argue from one to the other.

In Jefferson's Inaugural Address, where he develops what he calls "the essential principles of our government, and consequently those which ought to shape its administration," he mentions "*the supremacy of the civil over the military authority*" as one of these "essential principles," and then says: —

"These should be the creed of our political faith, — the text of civil instruction, — the touchstone by which to try the services of those we trust; and should we wander from them in moments of error or alarm, let us hasten to retrace our steps, and to regain the road which alone leads to peace, liberty, and safety."

In undertaking to create military governors of States, we reverse the policy of the republic, as solemnly declared by Jefferson, and subject the civil to the military authority. If this has been done, in patriotic ardor, without due consideration, in a moment of error or alarm, it only remains, that, according to Jefferson, we should "hasten to retrace our steps, and to regain the road which alone leads to peace, liberty, and safety."

There is nothing new under the sun, and the military governors whom we are beginning to appoint find a prototype in the Protectorate of Oliver Cromwell. After the execution of the King and the establishment of the Commonwealth, the Protector conceived the idea of parcelling the kingdom into military districts, of which there were *eleven*, — being precisely the number which it is now proposed, under the favor of success, to establish among us. Of this system a great authority, Mr. Hallam, in his "Constitutional History of England," speaks thus: —

"To govern according to law may sometimes be an usurper's wish, but can seldom be in his power. The Protector abandoned all thought of it. Dividing the kingdom into districts, he placed at the head of each a major-general, as *a sort of military magistrate*, responsible for the subjection of his prefecture. These were *eleven in number*, men bitterly hostile to the Royalist party, and insolent towards all civil authority." *

Carlyle, in his "Life of Cromwell," gives the following glimpse of this military government: —

"The beginning of a universal scheme of major-generals: the Lord-Protector and his Council of State having well considered and found it the feasiblest, — 'if not *good*, yet best.' 'It is an arbitrary government,' murmur many. Yes, arbitrary, but beneficial. *These are powers unknown to the English Constitution, I believe; but they are very necessary for the Puritan English nation at this time.*" †

Perhaps no better words could be found in explanation of the Cromwellian policy adopted by our President.

A contemporary Royalist, Colonel Ludlow, whose "Memoirs" add to our authentic history of those interesting times, characterizes these military magistrates as so many "bashaws." Here are some of his words: —

"The major-generals carried things with unheard-of insolence in their several precincts, decimating to extremity whom they pleased, and interrupting

* *Constitutional History of England*, Vol. II. p. 340.

† Carlyle's *Life of Cromwell*, Part IX. Vol. II. p. 168.

the proceedings at law upon petitions of those who pretended themselves aggrieved, *threatening such as would not yield a manly submission to their orders with transportation to Jamaica or some other plantation in the West Indies.*" *

Again, says the same contemporary writer : —

"There were sometimes bitter reflections cast upon the proceedings of the major-generals by the lawyers and country-gentlemen, who accused them to have done many things oppressive to the people, in interrupting the course of the law, and *threatening such as would not submit to their arbitrary orders with transportation beyond the seas.*" †

At last, even Cromwell, at the height of his power, found it necessary to abandon the policy of military governors. He authorized his son-in-law, Mr. Claypole, to announce in Parliament, "that he had formerly thought it necessary, in respect to the condition in which the nation had been, that the major-generals should be intrusted with the authority which they had exercised; but in the present state of affairs he conceived it inconsistent with the laws of England and liberties of the people to continue their power any longer." ‡

The conduct of at least one of our military magistrates seems to have been a counterpart to that of these "bashaws" of Cromwell; and there is no argument against that early military despotism which may not be urged against any attempt to revive it in our day. Some of the acts of Governor Stanley in North Carolina are in themselves an argument against the whole system.

It is clear that these military magistrates are without any direct sanction in the Constitution or in existing laws. They are not even "major-generals," or other military officers, charged with the duty of enforcing martial law; but they are special creations of the Secretary of War, acting under the President, and charged with universal powers. As governors within the limits of a State, they obviously assume the extinction of the old State governments for which they are substituted; and the President, in appointing them, assumes a power over these States kindred to his acknowledged power over Territories of the Union; but, in appointing governors for Territories, he acts in pursuance of the Constitution and laws, by and with the advice and consent of the Senate.

That the President should assume the vacation of the State governments is of itself no argument against the creation of military governors; for it is simply the assumption of an unquestionable fact. But if it be true that the State governments have ceased to exist, then the way is prepared for the establishment of provisional governments by Congress. In short, if a new government is to be supplied, it should be supplied by Congress rather than by the President, and it should be according to established law rather than according to the mere will of any functionary, to the end that ours may be a government of laws and not of men.

There is no argument for military governors which is not equally strong for Congressional governments, while the latter have in their favor two controlling considerations: first, that they proceed from the civil rather than the military power; and, secondly, that they are created by law. Therefore, in considering whether Congressional governments should be constituted, I begin the discussion by assuming everything in their favor which is already accorded to the other system. I should not do this, if the system of military dictators were not now recognized, so that the question is sharply presented, which of the two to choose. Even if provisional governments by Congress are not constitutional, it does not follow that military governments, without the sanction of Congress, can be constitutional. But, on the other hand, I cannot doubt, that, if military governments are constitutional, then, surely, the provisional governments by

* Ludlow's *Memoirs*, p. 559.

† *Ibid.* p. 580. ‡ *Ibid.* p. 582.

Congress must be so also. In truth, there can be no opening for military governments which is not also an opening for Congressional governments, with this great advantage for the latter, that they are in harmony with our institutions, which favor the civil rather than the military power.

In thus declaring an unhesitating preference for Congressional governments, I am obviously sustained by reason. But there is positive authority on this identical question. I refer to the recorded opinion of Chancellor Kent, as follows:—

"Though the Constitution vests the executive power in the President, and declares him Commander-in-Chief of the army and navy of the United States, *these powers must necessarily be subordinate to the legislative power in Congress.* It would appear to me to be the policy or true construction of this simple and general grant of power to the President, not to suffer it to interfere with those specific powers of Congress which are more safely deposited in the legislative department, and that *the powers thus assumed by the President do not belong to him, but to Congress.*" *

Such is the weighty testimony of this illustrious master with regard to the assumption of power by the President, in 1847, over the Mexican ports in our possession. It will be found in the latest edition of his "Commentaries" published during the author's life. Of course, it is equally applicable to the recent assumptions within our own territory. His judgment is clear in favor of Congressional governments.

Of course, in ordinary times, and under ordinary circumstances, neither system of government would be valid. A State, in the full enjoyment of its rights, would spurn a military governor or a Congressional governor. It would insist that its governor should be neither military nor Congressional, but such as its own people chose to elect; and nobody would question this right. The President does not think of sending a military governor to New York; nor does Congress think of establishing a provisional government in that State. It is only with regard to the Rebel States that this question arises. The occasion, then, for the exercise of this extraordinary power is found in the Rebellion. Without the Rebellion, there would be no talk of any governor, whether military or Congressional.

* Kent's *Commentaries*, Vol. I. p. 292, note *b*.

STATE RIGHTS.

And here it becomes important to consider the operation of the Rebellion in opening the way to this question. To this end we must understand the relations between the States and the National Government, under the Constitution of the United States. As I approach this question of singular delicacy, let me say on the threshold, that for all those rights of the States which are consistent with the peace, security, and permanence of the Union, according to the objects grandly announced in the Preamble of the Constitution, I am the strenuous advocate, at all times and places. Never through any word or act of mine shall those rights be impaired; nor shall any of those other rights be called in question by which the States are held in harmonious relations as well with each other as with the Union. But while thus strenuous for all that justly belongs to the States, I cannot concede to them immunities inconsistent with that Constitution which is the supreme law of the land; nor can I admit the impeccability of States.

From a period even anterior to the Federal Constitution there has been a perverse pretension of State Rights, which has perpetually interfered with the unity of our government. Throughout the Revolution this pretension was a check upon the powers of Congress, whether in respect to its armies or its finances; so that it was too often constrained to content itself with the language of advice or persuasion rather than of command. By the Declaration of Independence it was solemnly declared that "these United Colonies are, and of right ought to be, free and independent *States*, and that, as such, they have full powers to levy war, to contract alliances, to establish commerce, and to do all other acts which independent *States* may of right do." Thus by this original charter the early colonies were changed into independent States, under whose protection the liberties of the country were placed.

Early steps were taken to supply the deficiencies of this government, which was effective only through the generous patriotism of the people. In July, 1778, two years after the Declaration, Articles of Confederation were framed, but they were not completely ratified by all the States till March, 1781. The character of this new government, which assumed the style of "The United States of America," will appear in the title of these Articles, which was as follows: — "Articles of Confederation and Perpetual Union *between the States* of New Hampshire, Massachusetts Bay, Rhode Island and Providence Plantations, Connecticut, New York, New Jersey, Pennsylvania, Delaware, Maryland, Virginia, North Carolina, South Carolina, and Georgia." By the second article it was declared, that "*each State retains its sovereignty*, freedom, and independence, and every power, jurisdiction, and right which is not by this Confederation expressly delegated to the United States in Congress assembled." By the third article it was further declared, that "the said *States* hereby severally enter into *a firm league* of friendship with each other, for their common defence, the security of their liberties, and their mutual and general welfare." By another article, a "committee of the *States*, or any nine of them," was authorized in the recess to execute the powers of Congress. The government thus constituted was a compact between *sovereign States*, — or, according to its precise language, "a firm league of friendship" between *these States*, administered, in the recess of Congress, by a "committee of *the States*." Thus did State Rights triumph.

But its imbecility from this pretension soon became apparent. As early as December, 1782, a committee of Congress made an elaborate report on the refusal of Rhode Island, one of the States, to confer certain powers on Congress with regard to revenue and commerce. In April, 1783, an address of Congress to *the States* was put forth, appealing to their justice and plighted faith, and representing the consequence of a failure on their part to sustain the Government and provide for its wants. In April, 1784, a similar appeal was made to what were called "the several States," whose legislatures were recommended to vest "the United States in Congress assembled" with certain powers. In July, 1785, a committee of Congress made another elaborate report on the reason why the States should confer upon Congress powers therein enumerated, in the course of which it was urged, that, "unless *the States* act together, there is no plan of policy into which they can separately enter, which they will not be separately interested to defeat, and, of course, all their measures must prove vain and abortive." In February and March, 1786, there were two other reports of committees of Congress, exhibiting the failure of *the States* to comply with the requisitions of Congress, and the necessity for a complete accession of *all the States* to the revenue system. In October, 1786, there was still another report, most earnestly renewing the former appeals to *the States*. Nothing could be more urgent.

As early as July, 1782, even before the first report to Congress, resolutions were adopted by the State of New York, declaring "that the situation of *these States* is in a peculiar manner critical," and "that the radical source of most of our embarrassments is *the want of sufficient power in Congress* to effectuate that ready and perfect coöperation of *the different States* on which their immediate safety and future happiness depend." Finally, in September, 1786, at Annapolis, commissioners from several States, after declaring "the situation of the United States delicate and critical, calling for an exertion of the united virtue and wisdom of all the members of the Confederacy," recommended the meeting of a Convention "to devise such further provision as shall appear necessary to render the Constitution of the Federal Government adequate to the exigencies of the Union." In pursuance of this recommendation, the Congress of the Confederation proposed a Convention "for the purpose of revising the Articles of Confederation and Perpetual Union between the United States of America, and reporting such alterations and amendments of the said Articles of Confederation as the representatives met in such Convention shall judge proper and necessary to render them adequate to the preservation and support of the Union."

In pursuance of the call, delegates to the proposed Convention were duly appointed by the legislatures of the several States, and the Convention assembled at Philadelphia in May, 1787. The present Constitution was the well-ripened fruit of their deliberations. In transmitting it to Congress, General Washington, who was the President of the Convention, in a letter bearing date September 17, 1787, made use of this instructive language:—

"It is obviously impracticable in the Federal Government of *these States to secure all rights of independent sovereignty to each*, and yet provide for the interest and safety of all. Individuals entering into society must give up a share of liberty to preserve the rest. The magnitude of the sacrifice must depend as well on situation and circumstance as on the object to be obtained. It is at all times difficult to draw with precision the line between those rights which must be surrendered and those which may be reserved; and on the present occasion this difficulty will be increased by a difference *among the several States* as to their situation, extent, habits, and particular interests. In all our deliberations we kept steadily in view that which appears to us the greatest interest of every true American,—THE CONSOLIDATION OF OUR UNION,—in which is involved our prosperity, safety, perhaps our national existence.

"GEORGE WASHINGTON."

The Constitution was duly transmitted by Congress to the several legislatures, by which it was submitted to conventions of delegates "chosen in each State by the people thereof," who ratified the same. Afterwards, Congress, by resolution, dated September 13, 1788, setting forth that the Convention had reported "a Constitution *for the people of the United States*," which had been duly ratified, proceeded to authorize the necessary elections under the new government.

The Constitution, it will be seen, was framed in order to remove the difficulties arising from *State Rights*. So paramount was this purpose, that, according to the letter of Washington, it was kept steadily in view in all the deliberations of the Convention, which did not hesitate to declare *the consolidation of our Union* as essential to our prosperity, safety, and perhaps our national existence.

The unity of the government was expressed in the term "Constitution," instead of "Articles of Confederation between the States," and in the idea of "a more perfect union," instead of a "league of friendship." It was also announced emphatically in the Preamble:—

"*We, the people of the United States, in order to form a more perfect union*, establish justice, insure domestic tranquillity, provide for the common defence, promote the general welfare, and secure the blessings of liberty to ourselves and our posterity, do ordain and establish this Constitution for the United States of America."

Not "we, the States," but "we, the people of the United States." Such is the beginning and origin of our Constitution. Here is no compact or league between States, involving the recognition of State rights; but a government ordained and established by the people of the United States for themselves and their posterity. This government is not established *by the States*, nor is it established *for the States*; but it is established *by the people*, for themselves and their posterity. It is true, that, in the organization of the government, the existence of the States is recognized, and the original name of "United States" is preserved; but the sovereignty of the States is absorbed in that more perfect union which was then established. There is but one sovereignty recognized, and this is the sovereignty of the United States. To the several States is left that special local control which is essential to the convenience and business of life, while to the United States, as a *Plural Unit*, is allotted that commanding sovereignty which embraces and holds the whole country within its perpetual and irreversible jurisdiction.

This obvious character of the Constitution did not pass unobserved at the time of its adoption. Indeed, the Constitution was most strenuously opposed on the ground that the States were absorbed in the Nation. Patrick Henry protested against consolidated power. In the debates of the Virginia Convention he exclaimed: —

"And here I would make this inquiry of those worthy characters who composed a part of the late Federal Convention. I am sure they were fully impressed with the necessity of forming a great consolidated government, instead of a confederation. *That this is a consolidated government is demonstrably clear;* and the danger of such a government is to my mind very striking. I have the highest veneration for those gentlemen; but, Sir, give me leave to demand, What right had they to say, '*We, the people*'? Who authorized them to speak the language of '*We, the people*,' instead of '*We, the States*'?" *

And again, at another stage of the debate, the same patriotic opponent of the Constitution declared succinctly: —

"The question turns, Sir, on that poor little thing, the expression, 'We, *the people*,' instead of *the States* of America." *

In the same convention another patriotic opponent of the Constitution, George Mason, following Patrick Henry, said: —

"Whether the Constitution is good or bad, the present clause clearly discovers that it is a National Government, and no longer a Confederation." †

But against all this opposition, and in the face of this exposure, the Constitution was adopted, in the name of the people of the United States. Much, indeed, was left to the States; but it was no longer in their name that the government was organized, while the miserable pretension of State "sovereignty" was discarded. Even in the discussions of the Federal Convention Mr. Madison spoke thus plainly: —

"Some contend that States are *sovereign*, when, in fact, they are only political societies. The States never possessed the essential rights of sovereignty. These were always vested in Congress."

Grave words, especially when we consider the position of their author. They were substantially echoed by Elbridge Gerry of Massachusetts, afterwards Vice-President, who said: —

"It appears to me that the States never were independent. They had only corporate rights."

Better words still fell from Mr. Wilson of Pennsylvania, known afterwards as a learned judge of the Supreme Court, and also for his Lectures on Law: —

"Will a regard to State rights justify the sacrifice of the rights of men? If we proceed on any other foundation than the last, our building will neither be solid or lasting."

The argument was unanswerable then. It is unanswerable now. Do not elevate the sovereignty of the States against the Constitution of the United States. It is hardly less odious than the early pretension of sovereign power against Magna Charta, according to the memorable words

* Elliott's *Debates*, Vol. III. p. 22.

* Elliott's *Debates*, Vol. III. p. 44.

† *Ibid.* p. 29.

of Lord Coke, as recorded by Rushworth: —

"Sovereign power is no Parliamentary word. In my opinion, it weakens Magna Charta and all our statutes; for they are absolute without any saving of sovereign power. And shall we now add it, we shall weaken the foundation of law, and then the building must needs fall. Take we heed what we yield unto. *Magna Charta is such a fellow that he will have no sovereign.*" *

But the Constitution is our Magna Charta, which can bear no sovereign but itself, as you will see at once, if you will consider its character. And this practical truth was recognized at its formation, as may be seen in the writings of our Rushworth, — I refer to Nathan Dane, who was a member of Congress under the Confederation. He tells us plainly, that the terms "sovereign States," "State sovereignty," "State rights," "rights of States," are not "constitutional expressions."

POWERS OF CONGRESS.

In the exercise of its sovereignty Congress is intrusted with large and peculiar powers. Take notice of them, and you will see how little of "sovereignty" is left to the States. Their simple enumeration is an argument against the pretension of State Rights. Congress may lay and collect taxes, duties, imposts, and excises, to pay the debts and *provide for the common defence and general welfare of the United States.* It may borrow money on the credit of the United States; regulate commerce with foreign nations, and *among the several States*, and with the Indian tribes; establish a uniform rule of naturalization, and uniform laws on the subject of bankruptcy, *throughout the United States;* coin money, regulate the value thereof, and fix the standard of weights and measures; establish post-offices and post-roads; promote the progress of science and the useful arts by securing for limited times to authors and inventors the exclusive right to their respective writings and discoveries; define and punish piracies and felonies committed on the high seas, and offences against the law of nations; declare war; grant letters of marque and reprisal; make rules concerning captures on land and water; raise and support armies; provide and maintain a navy; make rules for the government and regulation of the land and naval forces; provide for calling forth the militia to execute *the laws of the Union*, suppress insurrections, and repel invasions; provide for organizing, arming, and disciplining the militia, and for governing such part of them as may be employed in the service of the United States, reserving to the States respectively the appointment of officers and the authority of training the militia *according to the discipline prescribed by Congress;* and make all laws necessary and proper for carrying into execution the foregoing powers and all other powers vested in the Government of the United States.

Such are the ample and diversified powers of Congress, embracing all those powers which enter into sovereignty. With the concession of these to the United States there seems to be little left for the several States. In the power to "declare war" and to "raise and support armies," Congress possesses an exclusive power, in itself immense and infinite, over persons and property in the several States, while by the power to "regulate commerce" it may put limits round about the business of the several States. And even in the case of the militia, which is the original military organization of the people, nothing is left to the States except "the appointment of the officers," and the authority to train it "according to the discipline *prescribed by Congress.*" It is thus that these great agencies are all intrusted to the United States, while the several States are subordinated to their exercise.

Constantly, and in everything, we behold the constitutional subordination of

* Rushworth's *Historical Collections*, Vol. I. p. 609.

the States. But there are other provisions by which the States are expressly deprived of important powers. For instance: "No State shall enter into any treaty, alliance, or confederation; coin money; emit bills of credit; make anything but gold and silver coin a tender in payment of debts." Or, if the States may exercise certain powers, it is only with the consent of Congress. For instance: "No State shall, *without the consent of Congress*, lay any duty of tonnage, keep troops or ships of war in time of peace, enter into any agreement or compact with another State or with a foreign power." Here is a magistral power accorded to Congress, utterly inconsistent with the pretensions of State Rights. Then, again: "No State shall, *without the consent of the Congress*, lay any imposts or duties on imports or exports, except what may be absolutely necessary for executing its inspection laws; and the net produce of all duties and imposts laid by any State on imports or exports shall be for the use of the treasury of the United States; *and all such laws shall be subject to the revision and control of the Congress.*" Here, again, is a similar magistral power accorded to Congress, and, as if still further to deprive the States of their much vaunted sovereignty, the laws which they make with the consent of Congress are expressly declared to be subject "to the revision and control of the Congress." But there is another instance still. According to the Constitution, "Full faith and credit shall be given in each State to the public acts, records, and judicial proceedings of every other State": but here mark the controlling power of Congress, which is authorized to "prescribe the manner in which such acts, records, and proceedings shall be proved, and the effect thereof."

SUPREMACY OF THE NATIONAL GOVERNMENT.

BUT there are five other provisions of the Constitution by which its supremacy is positively established. 1. "The citizens of each State shall be entitled to all privileges and immunities of citizens in the several States." As Congress has the exclusive power to establish "an uniform rule of naturalization," it may, under these words of the Constitution, secure for its newly entitled citizens "all privileges and immunities of citizens in the several States," in defiance of State Rights. 2. "New States may be admitted *by the Congress* into this Union." According to these words, the States cannot even determine their associates, but are dependent in this respect upon the will of Congress. 3. But not content with taking from the States these important powers of sovereignty, it is solemnly declared that the Constitution, and the laws of the United States made in pursuance thereof, and all treaties under the authority of the United States, "SHALL BE THE SUPREME LAW OF THE LAND, *anything in the Constitution or laws of any State to the contrary notwithstanding.*" Thus are State Rights again subordinated to the National Constitution, which is erected into the paramount authority. 4. But this is done again by another provision, which declares that "*the members of the several State legislatures*, and all executive and judicial officers of *the several States*, shall be bound by oath or affirmation to support this Constitution"; so that not only State laws are subordinated to the National Constitution, but the makers of State laws, and all other State officers, are constrained to declare their allegiance to this Constitution, thus placing the State, alike through its acts and its agents, in complete subordination to the sovereignty of the United States. 5. But this sovereignty is further proclaimed in the solemn injunction, that "the United States shall guarantee to every State in this Union a republican form of government, and shall protect each of them against invasion." Here are duties of guaranty and protection imposed upon the United States, by which their position is fixed as the supreme power. There can be no such guaranty without the implied right to examine and consider the governments of the several States; and there can be no such protection without a similar right to examine and consider the condition of the several States: thus subjecting them to the rightful supervision and superintendence of the National Government.

Thus, whether we regard the large powers vested in Congress, the powers denied to the States absolutely, the powers denied to the States without the consent of Congress, or those other provisions which accord supremacy to the United States, we shall find the pretension of State sovereignty without foundation, except in the imagination of its partisans. Before the Constitution such sovereignty may have existed; it was declared in the Articles of Confederation; but since then it has ceased to exist. It has disappeared and been lost in the supremacy of the National Government, so that it can no longer be recognized. Perverse men, insisting that it still existed, and weak men, mistaking the shadow of former power for the reality, have made arrogant claims in its behalf. When the Constitution was proclaimed, and George Washington took his oath to support it as President, our career as a Nation began, with all the unity of a nation. The States remained as living parts of the body, important to the national strength, and essential to those currents which maintain national life, but plainly subordinate to the United States, which then and there stood forth a Nation, one and indivisible.

MISCHIEFS IN THE NAME OF STATE RIGHTS.

BUT the new government had hardly been inaugurated before it was disturbed by the pestilent pretension of State Rights, which, indeed, has never ceased to disturb it since. Discontent with the treaty between the United States and Great Britain, negotiated by that purest patriot, John Jay, under instructions from Washington, in 1794, aroused Virginia, even at that early day, to commence an opposition to its ratification, *in the name of State Rights.* Shortly afterwards appeared the famous resolutions of Virginia and those of Kentucky, usually known as the "Resolutions of '98," declaring that the National Government was founded on a compact between the States, and claiming for the States the right to sit in judgment on the National Government, and to interpose, if they thought fit; all this, as you will see, *in the name of State Rights.* This pretension on the part of the States increased, till, at last, on the mild proposition to attach a prospective prohibition of Slavery as a condition to the admission of Missouri into the Union as a new State, the opposition raged furiously, even to the extent of menacing the existence of the Union; and this, too, was done *in the name of State Rights.* Ten years later, the pretension took the familiar form of Nullification, insisting that our government was only a compact of States, any one of which was free to annul an act of Congress at its own pleasure; and all this *in the name of State Rights.* For a succession of years afterwards, at the presentation of petitions against Slavery, — petitions for the recognition of Hayti, — at the question of Texas, — at the Wilmot Proviso, — at the admission of California as a Free State, — at the discussion of the Compromises of 1850, — at the Kansas Question, — the Union was menaced; and always *in the name of State Rights.* The menace was constant, and it sometimes showed itself on small as well as great occasions, but always *in the name of State Rights.* When it was supposed that Fremont was about to be chosen President, the menace became louder, and mingling with it was the hoarse mutter of war; and all this audacity was *in the name of State Rights.*

But in the autumn of 1860, on the election of Mr. Lincoln, the case became much worse. Scarcely was the result of this election known by telegraph before the country was startled by other intelligence, to the effect that certain States at the South were about to put in execution the long-pending threat of Secession, of course *in the name of State Rights.* First came South Carolina, which, by an ordinance adopted in a State convention, undertook to repeal the original act by which the Constitution was adopted in this State, and to declare that the State had ceased to be one of the States of the Union. At the same time a Declaration of Independence was put forth by this State, which proceeded to organize itself as an independent community. This example was followed successively by other States, which, by formal acts of Secession, undertook to dissolve their relations with the Union, always, be it understood, *in the name of State Rights.* A new Confederation was formed by these States, with a new Constitution, and Jefferson Davis at its head; and the same oaths of loyalty by which the local functionaries of all these States had been bound to the Union were now transferred to this new Confederation, — of course, in utter violation of the Constitution of the United States, but always *in the name of State Rights.* The ordinances of Secession were next maintained by war, which, beginning with the assault upon Fort Sumter, convulsed the whole country, till, at last, all the States of the new Confederation are in open rebellion, which the Government of the United States is now exerting its energies, mustering its forces, and taxing its people to suppress. The original claim, *in the name of State Rights*, has swollen to all the proportions of an unparalleled war, which, *in the name of State Rights*, now menaces the national life.

But the pretensions in the name of State Rights are not all told. While the ordinances of Secession were maturing, and before they were yet consummated, Mr. Buchanan, who was then President, declined to interfere, on the ground that what had been done was done by States, and that it was contrary to the theory of our government "to coerce a State." Thus was the pretension of State Rights made the apology for imbecility. Had this President then interfered promptly and loyally, it cannot be doubted that this whole intolerable crime might have been trampled out forever. And now, when it is proposed that Congress shall organize governments in these States, which are absolutely without loyal governments, we are met by the objection founded on State Rights. The same disastrous voice which from the beginning of our history has sounded in our ears still makes itself heard; but, alas! it is now on the lips of our friends. Of course, just in proportion as it prevails will it be impossible to establish the Constitution again throughout the Rebel States. State Rights are madly triumphant, if, first, in their name Rebel governments can be organized, and then, again, in their name Congressional governments to displace the Rebel governments can be resisted. If they can be employed, first to sever the States from the Union, and then to prevent the Union from extending its power over them, State Rights are at once a sword and buckler to the Rebellion. It was through the imbecility of Mr. Buchanan that the States were allowed to use the sword. God forbid that now, through any similar imbecility of Congress, they shall be allowed to use the buckler!

SHALL CONGRESS ASSUME JURISDICTION OF THE REBEL STATES?

AND now, in this discussion, we are brought to the practical question which is destined to occupy so much of public attention. It is proposed to bring the action of Congress to bear directly upon the Rebel States. This may be by the establishment of provisional governments under the authority of Congress, or simply by making the admission or recognition of the States depend upon the action of Congress. The essential feature of this proposition is, *that Congress shall assume jurisdiction of the Rebel States.* A bill authorizing provisional governments in these States was introduced into the Senate by Mr.

Harris of the State of New York, and was afterwards reported from the Judiciary Committee of that body; but it was left with the unfinished business, when the late Congress expired on the fourth of March. The opposition to this proposition, so far as I understand it, assumes two forms: first, that these States are always to be regarded as States, with State rights, and therefore cannot be governed by Congress; and, secondly, that, if any government is to be established over them, it must be simply a military government, with a military governor, appointed by the President, as is the case with Tennessee and North Carolina. But State rights are as much disturbed by a military government as by a Congressional government. The local government is as much set aside in one case as in the other. If the President, within State limits, can proceed to organize a military government to exercise all the powers of the State, surely Congress can proceed to organize a civil government within the same limits for the same purpose; nor can any pretension of State Rights be effective against Congress more than against the President. Indeed, the power belongs to Congress by a higher title than it belongs to the President: first, because a civil government is more in harmony with our institutions, and, wherever possible, is required; and, secondly, because there are provisions of the Constitution under which this power is clearly derived.

Assuming, then, that the pretension of State Rights is as valid against one form of government as against the other, and still further assuming, that, in the case of military governments, this pretension is practically overruled by the President at least, we are brought again to consider the efficacy of this pretension when advanced against Congressional governments.

It is argued that the Acts of Secession are all inoperative and void, and that therefore the States continue precisely as before, with their local constitutions, laws, and institutions in the hands of traitors, but totally unchanged, and ready to be quickened into life by returning loyalty. Such, I believe, is a candid statement of the pretension for State Rights against Congressional governments, which, it is argued, cannot be substituted for the State governments.

In order to prove that the Rebel States continue precisely as before, we are reminded that Andrew Johnson continued to occupy his seat in the Senate after Tennessee had adopted its Act of Secession and embarked in rebellion, and that his presence testified to the fact that Rebel Tennessee was still a State of the Union. No such conclusion is authorized by the incident in question. There are two principles of Parliamentary law long ago fixed: first, that the power once conferred by an election to Parliament is *irrevocable*, so that it is not affected by any subsequent change in the constituency; and, secondly, that a member, when once chosen, is *a member for the whole kingdom*, becoming thereby, according to the words of an early author, not merely knight or burgess of the county or borough which elected him, but knight or burgess of England.* If these two principles are not entirely inapplicable to our political system, then the seat of Andrew Johnson was not in any respect affected by the subsequent madness of his State, nor can the legality of his seat be any argument for his State.

We are also reminded that during the last session of Congress two Senators from Virginia represented that State in the Senate; and the argument is pressed, that no such representation would be valid, if the State government of Virginia was vacated. This is a mistake. Two things are established by the presence of these Senators in the National Senate: first, that the old State government of Virginia is extinct, and, secondly, that a new government has been set up in its place. It was my fortune to listen to one of these Senators while he earnestly denounced the idea

* See Cushing, *Parliamentary Law*, p. 284.

that a State government might disappear. I could not but think that he strangely forgot the principle to which he owed his seat in the Senate, — as men sometimes forget a benefactor.

It is true, beyond question, that the Acts of Secession are all inoperative and void against the Constitution of the United States. Though matured in successive conventions, sanctioned in various forms, and maintained ever since by bloody war, these acts — no matter by what name they may be called — are all equally impotent to withdraw an acre of territory or a single inhabitant from the rightful jurisdiction of the United States. But while thus impotent against the United States, it does not follow that they were equally impotent in the work of self-destruction. Clearly, the Rebels, by utmost efforts, could not impair the National jurisdiction; but it remains to be seen if their enmity did not act back with fatal rebound upon those very State Rights in behalf of which they commenced their treason.

STATE SUICIDE.

It is sometimes said that the States themselves committed *suicide*, so that as States they ceased to exist, leaving their whole jurisdiction open to the occupation of the United States under the Constitution. This assumption is founded on the fact, that, whatever may be the existing governments in these States, they are in no respect constitutional, and since the State itself is known by the government, with which its life is intertwined, it must cease to exist constitutionally when its government no longer exists constitutionally. Perhaps, however, it would be better to avoid the whole question of the life or death of the State, and to content ourselves with an inquiry into the condition of its government. It is not easy to say what constitutes that entity which we call a State; nor is the discussion much advanced by any theory with regard to it. To my mind it seems a topic fit for the old schoolmen or a modern debating society; and yet, considering the part it has already played in this discussion, I shall be pardoned for a brief allusion to it.

There are well-known words which ask and answer the question, "What constitutes *a State?*" But the scholarly poet was not thinking of a "State" of the American Union. Indeed, this term is various in its use. Sometimes it stands for civil society itself. Sometimes it is the general name for a political community, not unlike "nation" or "country," — as where our fathers, in the Resolution of Independence, which preceded the Declaration, spoke of "the *State* of Great Britain." Sometimes it stands for the government, — as when Louis XIV., at the height of his power, exclaimed, "The *State*, it is I"; or when Sir Christopher Hatton, in the famous farce of "The Critic," ejaculates, —

> "Oh, pardon me, if my conjecture 's rash,
> But I surmise —— *the State* ——
> Some danger apprehends."

Among us the term is most known as the technical name for one of the political societies which compose our Union. Of course, when used in the latter restricted sense, it must not be confounded with the same term when used in a different and broader sense. But it is obvious that some persons attribute to the one something of the qualities which can belong only to the other. Nobody has suggested, I presume, that any "State" of our Union has, through rebellion, ceased to exist as a *civil society*, or even as a *political community*. It is only as a *State of the Union*, armed with State rights, or at least as a *local government*, which annually renews itself, as the snake its skin, that it can be called in question. But it is vain to challenge for the technical "State," or for the annual government, that immortality which belongs to civil society. The one is an artificial body, the other is a natural body; and while the first, overwhelmed by insurrection or war, may change or die, the latter can change or die only with the extinction of the community itself, whatever may be its name or its form.

It is because of confusion in the use of this term that there has been so much confusion in the political controversies where it has been employed. But nowhere has this confusion led to greater absurdity than in the pretension which has been recently made in the name of State Rights, — as if it were reasonable to attribute to a technical " State " of the Union that immortality which belongs to civil society.

From approved authorities it appears that a " State," even in a broader signification, may lose its life. Mr. Phillimore, in his recent work on International Law, says:—" A State, like an individual, may die," and among the various ways, he says, " by its submission and the donation of itself to another country." * But in the case of our Rebel States there has been a plain submission and donation of themselves, — *effective, at least, to break the continuity of government*, if not to destroy that immortality which has been claimed. Nor can it make any difference, in breaking this continuity, that the submission and donation, constituting a species of attornment, were to enemies at home rather than to enemies abroad, — to Jefferson Davis rather than to Louis Napoleon. The thread is snapped in one case as much as in the other.

But a *change of form* in the actual government may be equally effective. Cicero speaks of a change so complete as " to leave no image of a State behind." But this is precisely what has been done throughout the whole Rebel region : there is no image of a *constitutional* State left behind. Another authority, Aristotle, whose words are always weighty, says, that, *the form of the State being changed, the State is no longer the same*, as the harmony is not the same when we modulate out of the Dorian mood into the Phrygian. But if ever an unlucky people modulated out of one mood into another, it was our Rebels, when they undertook to modulate out of the harmonies of the Constitution into their bloody discords.

Without stopping further for these diversions, I content myself with the testimony of Edmund Burke, who, in a striking passage, which seems to have been written for us, portrays the extinction of a political community; but I quote his eloquent words rather for suggestion than for authority : —

" In a state of *rude* Nature there is no such thing as a people. A number of men in themselves have no collective capacity. The idea of people is the idea of a corporation. It is wholly artificial, and made, like all other legal fictions, by common agreement. What the particular nature of that agreement was is collected from the form into which the particular society has been cast. Any other is not *their* covenant. *When men, therefore, break up the original compact or agreement which gives its corporate form and capacity to a State, they are no longer a people; they have no longer a corporate existence;* they have no longer a legal coactive force to bind within, nor a claim to be recognized abroad. They are a number of vague, loose individuals, and nothing more. With them all is to begin again. Alas ! they little know how many a weary step is to be taken before they can form themselves into a mass which has a true politic personality." *

If that great master of eloquence could be heard, who can doubt that he would blast our Rebel States, as senseless communities who have sacrificed that corporate existence which makes them living, component members of our Union of States ?

STATE FORFEITURE.

But again it is sometimes said, that the States, by their flagrant treason, have *forfeited* their rights as States, so as to be civilly dead. It is a patent and indisputable fact, that this gigantic treason was inaugurated with all the forms of

* Phillimore's *International Law*, Vol. I. p. 147.

* Burke's *Appeal from the New to the Old Whigs.*

law known to the States; that it was carried forward not only by individuals, but also by States, so far as States can perpetrate treason; that the States pretended to withdraw bodily in their corporate capacities;—that the Rebellion, as it showed itself, was *by* States as well as *in* States; that it was by the governments of States as well as by the people of States; and that, to the common observer, the crime was consummated by the several corporations as well as by the individuals of whom they were composed. From this fact, obvious to all, it is argued, that, since, according to Blackstone, "a traitor hath abandoned his connection with society, and hath no longer any right to the advantages which before belonged to him purely as a member of the community," by the same principle the traitor State is no longer to be regarded as a member of the Union. But it is not necessary, on the present occasion, to insist on the application of any such principle to States.

STATE ABDICATION.

AGAIN it is said, that the States by their treason and rebellion, levying war upon the National Government, have *abdicated* their places in the Union; and here the argument is upheld by the historic example of England, at the Revolution of 1688, when, on the flight of James II. and the abandonment of his kingly duties, the two Houses of Parliament voted, that the monarch, "having violated the fundamental laws, and having withdrawn himself out of the kingdom, *had abdicated the government*, and that the throne had thereby become vacant."* But it is not necessary for us to rely on any allegation of abdication, applicable as it may be.

RIGHTFUL GOVERNMENT IN THE REBEL STATES VACATED.

IT only remains that we should see things as they are, and not seek to substitute theory for fact. On this important question I discard all theory, whether it be of State suicide or State forfeiture or State abdication, on the one side, or of State rights, immortal and unimpeachable, on the other side. Such discussions are only endless mazes in which a whole senate may be lost. And in discarding all theory, I discard also the question of *de jure*,—whether, for instance, the Rebel States, while the Rebellion is flagrant, are *de jure* States of the Union, with all the rights of States. It is enough, that, for the time being, and *in the absence of a loyal government*, they can take no part and perform no function in the Union, *so that they cannot be recognized by the National Government.* The reason is plain. There are in these States no local functionaries bound by constitutional oaths, so that, in fact, there are no constitutional functionaries; and since the State government is necessarily composed of such functionaries, there can be no State government. Thus, for instance, in South Carolina, Pickens and his associates may call themselves the governor and legislature, and in Virginia, Letcher and his associates may call themselves governor and legislature; but we cannot recognize them as such. Therefore to all pretensions in behalf of State governments in the Rebel States I oppose the simple FACT, that for the time being no such governments exist. The broad spaces once occupied by those governments are now abandoned and vacated.

That patriot Senator, Andrew Johnson,—faithful among the faithless, the Abdiel of the South,—began his attempt to reorganize Tennessee by an Address, as early as the 18th of March, 1862, in which he made use of these words:—

"I find most, if not all, of the offices, both State and Federal, *vacated, either by actual abandonment, or by the action of the incumbents in attempting to subordinate their functions* to a power in hostility to the fundamental law of the State and subversive of her national allegiance."

In employing the word "vacated," Mr.

* Macaulay's *History of England*, Vol. II. p. 623.

Johnson hit upon the very term which, in the famous resolution of 1688, was held to be most effective in dethroning King James. After declaring that he had abdicated the government, it was added, "that the throne had thereby become *vacant*," on which Macaulay happily remarks: —

"The word *abdication* conciliated politicians of a more timid school. To the real statesman the simple important clause was that *which declared the throne vacant;* and if that clause could be carried, he cared little by what preamble it might be introduced." *

And the same simple principle is now in issue. It is enough that the Rebel States be declared *vacated*, as *in fact* they are, by all local government which we are bound to recognize, so that the way is open to the exercise of a rightful jurisdiction.

TRANSITION TO RIGHTFUL GOVERNMENT.

AND here the question occurs, How shall this rightful jurisdiction be established in the vacated States? Some there are, so impassioned for State rights, and so anxious for forms even at the expense of substance, that they insist upon the instant restoration of the old State governments in all their parts, through the agency of loyal citizens, who meanwhile must be protected in this work of restoration. But, assuming that all this is practicable, as it clearly is not, it attributes to the loyal citizens of a Rebel State, however few in numbers, — it may be an insignificant minority, — a power clearly inconsistent with the received principle of popular government, that the majority must rule. The seven voters of Old Sarum were allowed to return two members of Parliament, because this place, — once a Roman fort, and afterwards a sheepwalk, — many generations before, at the early casting of the House of Commons, had been entitled to this representation; but the argument for State Rights assumes that all these rights may be lodged in voters as few in number as ever controlled a rotten borough of England.

Pray, admitting that an insignificant minority is to organize the new government, how shall it be done? and by whom shall it be set in motion? In putting these questions I open the difficulties. As the original government has ceased to exist, and there are none who can be its legal successors, so as to administer the requisite oaths, it is not easy to see how the new government can be set in motion without a resort to some revolutionary proceeding, instituted either by the citizens or by the military power, — unless Congress, in the exercise of its plenary powers, should undertake to organize the new jurisdiction.

But every revolutionary proceeding is to be avoided. It will be within the recollection of all familiar with our history, that our fathers, while regulating the separation of the Colonies from the parent country, were careful that all should be done according to the forms of law, so that the thread of *legality* should continue unbroken. To this end the Continental Congress interfered by a supervising direction. But the Tory argument in that day denied the power of Congress as earnestly as it denies this power now. Mr. Duane, of the Continental Congress, made himself the mouthpiece of this denial: —

"*Congress ought not to determine a point of this sort about instituting government.* What is it to Congress how justice is administered? You have no right to pass the resolution, any more than Parliament has. How does it appear that no favorable answer is likely to be given to our petitions?" *

In spite of this argument, the Congress of that day undertook, by formal resolutions, to indicate the process by which the new governments should be constituted.†

* Macaulay's *History of England*, Vol. II. p. 624.

* John Adams's *Works*, Vol. II. p. 490.

† *Ibid.* Vol. III. pp. 17, 19, 45, 46.

If we seek, for our guidance, the principle which entered into this proceeding of the Continental Congress, we shall find it in the idea, that nothing must be left to illegal or informal action, but that all must be done according to rules of constitution and law previously ordained. Perhaps this principle has never been more distinctly or powerfully enunciated than by Mr. Webster, in his speech against the Dorr Constitution in Rhode Island. According to him, this principle is a fundamental part of what he calls our American system, requiring that the right of suffrage shall be prescribed by *previous law*, including its qualifications, the time and place of its exercise, and the manner of its exercise; and then again, that the results are to be certified to the central power by some certain rule, *by some known public officers*, in some clear and definite form, to the end that two things may be done: first, that every man entitled to vote may vote; secondly, that his vote may be sent forward and counted, and so he may exercise his part of sovereignty, in common with his fellow-citizens. Such, according to Mr. Webster, are the minute forms which must be followed, if we would impart to the result the crowning character of law. And here are other positive words from him on this important point: —

"We are not to take the will of the people from public meetings, nor from tumultuous assemblies, by which the timid are terrified, the prudent are alarmed, and by which society is disturbed. These are not American modes of signifying the will of the people, and they never were. . . . .

"Is it not obvious enough, that men cannot get together and count themselves, and say they are so many hundreds and so many thousands, and judge of their own qualifications, and call themselves the people, and set up a government? *Why, another set of men, forty miles off, on the same day, with the same propriety, with as good qualifications, and in as large numbers, may meet and set up another government.* . . . .

"When, in the course of human events, it becomes necessary to ascertain the will of the people on a new exigency, or a new state of things, or of opinion, *the legislative power provides for that ascertainment by an ordinary act of legislation.*

"What do I contend for? I say that the will of the people must prevail, when it is ascertained; but there must be *some legal and authentic mode of ascertaining that will;* and then the people may make what government they please. . . . .

"All that is necessary here is, that the will of the people should be ascertained by some regular rule of proceeding, *prescribed by previous law.* . . . .

"But the law and the Constitution, the whole system of American institutions, do not contemplate a case in which a resort will be necessary to proceedings *aliunde*, or *outside of the law and the Constitution*, for the purpose of amending the frame of government." *

CONGRESS THE TRUE AGENT.

But, happily, we are not constrained to any such revolutionary proceeding. The new governments can all be organized by Congress, which is the natural guardian of people without any immediate government, and within the jurisdiction of the Constitution of the United States. Indeed, with the State governments already *vacated* by rebellion, the Constitution becomes, for the time, the supreme and only law, binding alike on President and Congress, so that neither can establish any law or institution incompatible with it. And the whole Rebel region, deprived of all local government, lapses under the exclusive jurisdiction of Congress, precisely as any other territory; or, in other words, the lifting of the local governments leaves the whole vast region without any other government than Congress, unless the President should undertake to govern it by military power. Startling as this proposition may seem, especially

* Webster's *Works*, Vol. VI. pp. 225, 226, 227, 228, 231.

to all who believe that "there is a divinity that doth hedge" a State, hardly less than a king, it will appear, on careful consideration, to be as well founded in the Constitution as it is simple and natural, while it affords an easy and constitutional solution to our present embarrassments.

I have no theory to maintain, but only the truth; and in presenting this argument for Congressional government, I simply follow teachings which I cannot control. The wisdom of Socrates, in the words of Plato, has aptly described these teachings, when he says: —

"These things are secured and bound, even if the expression be somewhat too rude, with iron and adamant; and unless you or some one more vigorous than you can break them, it is impossible for any one speaking otherwise than I now speak to speak well; since, for my part, I have always the same thing to say, that I know not how these things are, but that out of all with whom I have ever discoursed, as now, not one is able to say otherwise and to maintain himself." *

Show me that I am wrong, — that this conclusion is not founded in the Constitution, and is not sustained by reason, — and I shall at once renounce it; for, in the present condition of affairs, there can be no pride of opinion which must not fall at once before the sacred demands of country. Not as a partisan, not as an advocate, do I make this appeal; but simply as a citizen, who seeks, in all sincerity, to offer his contribution to the establishment of that policy by which Union and Peace may be restored.

THREE SOURCES OF CONGRESSIONAL POWER.

If we look at the origin of this power in Congress, we shall find that it comes from three distinct fountains, any one of which is ample to supply it. Three fountains, generous and hospitable, will be found in the Constitution ready for this occasion.

* The *Gorgias* of Plato.

First. From the necessity of the case, *ex necessitate rei*, Congress must have jurisdiction over every portion of the United States *where there is no other government*; and since in the present case there is no other government, the whole region falls within the jurisdiction of Congress. This jurisdiction is incident, if you please, to that guardianship and eminent domain which belong to the United States with regard to all its territory and the people thereof, and it comes into activity when the local government ceases to exist. It can be questioned only in the name of the local government; but since this government has disappeared in the Rebel States, the jurisdiction of Congress is uninterrupted there. The whole broad Rebel region is *tabula rasa*, or "a clean slate," where Congress, under the Constitution of the United States, may write the laws. In adopting this principle, I follow the authority of the Supreme Court of the United States in determining the jurisdiction of Congress over the Territories. Here are the words of Chief-Justice Marshall: —

"Perhaps the power of governing a territory belonging to the United States, which has not, by becoming a State, acquired the means of self-government, *may result necessarily from the facts that it is not within the jurisdiction of any particular State* and is within the power and jurisdiction of the United States. The right to govern may be the natural consequence of the right to acquire territory." *

If the right to govern may be the natural consequence of the right to acquire territory, surely, and by much stronger reason, this right must be the natural consequence of the sovereignty of the United States wherever there is no local government.

Secondly. This jurisdiction may also be derived from the *Rights of War*, which surely are not less abundant for Congress than for the President. If the Presi-

* *American Insurance Company* v. *Carter*, 1 Peters, p. 542.

dent, disregarding the pretension of State Rights, can appoint military governors within the Rebel States, to serve a temporary purpose, who can doubt that Congress can exercise a similar jurisdiction? That of the President is derived from the war-powers; but these are not sealed to Congress. If it be asked where in the Constitution such powers are bestowed upon Congress, I reply, that they will be found precisely where the President now finds his powers. But it is clear that the powers to "declare war," to "suppress insurrections," and to "support armies," are all ample for this purpose. It is Congress that conquers; and the same authority that conquers must govern. Nor is this authority derived from any strained construction; but it springs from the very heart of the Constitution. It is among those powers, latent in peace, which war and insurrection call into being, but which are as intrinsically constitutional as any other power.

Even if not conceded to the President, these powers must be conceded to Congress. Would you know their extent? They will be found in the authoritative texts of Public Law, — in the works of Grotius, Vattel, and Wheaton. They are the powers conceded by civilized society to nations at war, known as the Rights of War, at once multitudinous and minute, vast and various. It would be strange, if Congress could organize armies and navies to conquer, and could not also organize governments to protect.

De Tocqueville, who saw our institutions with so keen an eye, remarked, that, since, in spite of all political fictions, the preponderating power resided in the State governments, and not in the National Government, a civil war here "would be nothing but a foreign war in disguise."* Of course the natural consequence would be to give the National Government in such a civil war all the rights which it would have in a foreign war. And this conclusion from the observation of the ingenious publicist has been practically adopted by the Supreme Court of the United States in those recent cases where this tribunal, after the most learned argument, followed by the most careful consideration, adjudged, that, since the Act of Congress of July 13th, 1861, the National Government has been waging "a *territorial* civil war," in which all property afloat belonging to a resident of the *belligerent territory* is liable to capture and condemnation as lawful prize. But surely, if the National Government may stamp upon all residents in this *belligerent territory* the character of foreign enemies, so as to subject their ships and cargoes to the penalties of confiscation, it may perform the milder service of making all needful rules and regulations for the government of this territory under the Constitution, so long as may be requisite for the sake of peace and order; and since the object of war is "indemnity for the past and security for the future," it may do everything necessary to make these effectual. But it will not be enough to crush the Rebellion. Its terrible root must be exterminated, so that it may no more flaunt in blood.

Thirdly. But there is another source for this jurisdiction which is common alike to Congress and the President. It will be found in the constitutional provision, that "the United States shall guarantee to every State in this Union a republican form of government, and shall protect each of them against invasion." Here, be it observed, are words of guaranty and an obligation of protection. In the original concession to the United States of this twofold power there was an open recognition of the ultimate responsibility and duty of the National Government, *conferring jurisdiction above all pretended State rights;* and now the occasion has come for the exercise of this twofold power thus solemnly conceded. The words of twofold power and corresponding obligation are plain and beyond question. If there be any ambiguity, it is only as to what constitutes a republican form

* *Democracy in America*, Vol. II. ch. 25, p. 343.

of government. But for the present this question does not arise. It is enough that a wicked rebellion has undertaken to detach certain States from the Union, and to take them beyond the protection and sovereignty of the United States, with the menace of seeking foreign alliance and support, even at the cost of every distinctive institution. It is well known that *Mr. Madison anticipated this precise danger from Slavery, and upheld this precise grant of power in order to counteract this danger.* His words, which will be found in a yet unpublished document, produced by Mr. Collamer in the Senate, seem prophetic.

Among the defects which he remarked in the old Confederation was what he called "want of guaranty to the States of their constitutions and laws *against internal violence.*" In showing why this guaranty was needed, he says, that, "according to republican theory, right and power, being both vested in the majority, are held to be synonymous; according to fact and experience, a minority may, in an appeal to force, be an overmatch for the majority"; and he then adds, in words of wonderful prescience, "*where Slavery exists the republican theory becomes still more fallacious.*" This was written in April, 1787, before the meeting of the Convention that formed the National Constitution. But here we have the origin of the very clause in question. The danger which this statesman foresaw is now upon us. When a State fails to maintain a republican government *with officers sworn according to the requirements of the Constitution*, it ceases to be a constitutional State. The very case contemplated by the Constitution has arrived, and the National Government is invested with plenary powers, whether of peace or war. There is nothing in the storehouse of peace, and there is nothing in the arsenal of war, which it may not employ in the maintenance of this solemn guaranty, and in the extension of that protection against invasion to which it is pledged. But this extraordinary power carries with it a corresponding duty. Whatever shows itself dangerous to a republican form of government must be removed without delay or hesitation; and if the evil be Slavery, our action will be bolder when it is known that the danger was foreseen.

In reviewing these three sources of power, I know not which is most complete. Either would be ample alone; but the three together are three times ample. Thus, out of this triple fountain, or, if you please, by this triple cord, do I vindicate the power of Congress over the vacated Rebel States.

But there are yet other words of the Constitution which cannot be forgotten: "New States may be admitted by the Congress into this Union." Assuming that the Rebel States are no longer *de facto* States of this Union, but that the territory occupied by them is within the jurisdiction of Congress, then these words become completely applicable. It will be for Congress, in such way as it shall think best, to regulate the return of these States to the Union, whether in time or manner. No special form is prescribed. But the vital act must proceed from Congress. And here again is another testimony to that Congressional power which, under the Constitution, will restore the Republic.

UNANSWERABLE REASONS FOR CONGRESSIONAL GOVERNMENTS.

Against this power I have heard no argument which can be called an argument. There are objections founded chiefly in the baneful pretension of State Rights; but these objections are animated by prejudice rather than reason. Assuming the impeccability of the States, and openly declaring that States, like kings, can do no wrong, while, like kings, they wear the "round and top of sovereignty," politicians treat them with most mistaken forbearance and tenderness, as if these Rebel corporations could be dandled into loyalty. At every suggestion of rigor State Rights are invoked, and we are vehemently told not to destroy the States, when all that Congress proposes is simply to recognize the actual condition of the States and to undertake their temporary government, by providing for the condition of political syncope into which they have fallen, and, during this interval, to substitute its own constitutional powers for the unconstitutional powers of the Rebellion. Of course, therefore, Congress will blot no star from the flag, nor will it obliterate any State liabilities. But it will seek, according to its duty, in the best way, to maintain the great and real sovereignty of the Union, by upholding the flag unsullied, and by enforcing everywhere within its jurisdiction the supreme law of the Constitution.

At the close of an argument already too long drawn out, I shall not stop to array the considerations of reason and expediency in behalf of this jurisdiction; nor shall I dwell on the inevitable influence that it must exercise over Slavery, which is the motive of the Rebellion. To my mind nothing can be clearer, as a proposition of constitutional law, than that everywhere within the exclusive jurisdiction of the National Government Slavery is impossible. The argument is as brief as it is unanswerable. Slavery is so odious that it can exist only by virtue of positive law, plain and unequivocal; but no such words can be found in the Constitution. Therefore Slavery is impossible within the exclusive jurisdiction of the National Government. For many years I have had this conviction, and have constantly maintained it. I am glad to believe that it is implied, if not expressed, in the Chicago Platform. Mr. Chase, among our public men, is known to accept it sincerely. Thus Slavery in the Territories is unconstitutional; but if the Rebel territory falls under the exclusive jurisdiction of the National Government, then Slavery will be impossible there. In a legal and constitutional sense, it will die at once. The air will be too pure for a slave. I cannot doubt that this great triumph has been already won. The moment that the States fell, Slavery fell also; so that, even without any Proclamation of the President, Slavery had ceased to have a legal and constitutional existence in every Rebel State.

But even if we hesitate to accept this important conclusion, which treats Slavery within the Rebel States as already dead in law and Constitution, it cannot be doubted, that, by the extension of the Congressional jurisdiction over the Rebel States, many difficulties will be removed. Holding every acre of soil and every inhabitant of these States within its jurisdiction, Congress can easily do, by proper legislation, whatever may be needful within Rebel limits in order to assure freedom and to save society. The soil may be divided among patriot soldiers, poor-whites, and freedmen. But above all things, the inhabitants may be saved from harm. Those citizens in the Rebel States, who, throughout the darkness of the Rebellion, have kept their faith, will be protected, and the freedmen will be rescued from hands that threaten to cast them back into Slavery.

But this jurisdiction, which is so completely practical, is grandly conservative also. Had it been early recognized that Slavery depends exclusively upon the local government, and that it falls with that government, who can doubt that every Rebel movement would have been checked? Tennessee and Virginia would never have stirred; Maryland and Kentucky would never have thought of stirring. There would have been no talk of neutrality between the Constitution and the Rebellion, and every Border State would have been fixed in its loyalty. Let it be established in advance, as an inseparable incident to every Act of Secession, that it is not only impotent against the Constitution of the United States, but that, on its occurrence, both soil and inhabitants will lapse beneath the jurisdiction of Congress, and no State will ever again pretend to secede. The word "territory," according to an old and quaint etymology, is said to come from *terreo*, to terrify, because it was a bulwark against the enemy. A scholiast tells us, "*Territorium est quic-*

quid hostis terrendi causâ constitutum," "A territory is something constituted in order to terrify the enemy." But I know of no way in which our Rebel enemy would have been more terrified than by being told that his course would inevitably precipitate him into a territorial condition. Let this principle be adopted now, and it will contribute essentially to that consolidation of the Union which was so near the heart of Washington.

The necessity of this principle is apparent as a restraint upon the lawless vindictiveness and inhumanity of the Rebel States, whether against Union men or against freedmen. Union men in Virginia already tremble at the thought of being delivered over to a State government wielded by original Rebels pretending to be patriots. But the freedmen, who have only recently gained their birthright, are justified in a keener anxiety, lest it should be lost as soon as won. Mr. Saulsbury, a Senator from Delaware, with most instructive frankness, has announced, in public debate, what the restored State governments will do. Assuming that the local governments will be preserved, he predicts that in 1870 there will be more slaves in the United States than there were in 1860, and then unfolds the reason as follows, — all of which will be found in the "Congressional Globe"*: —

"By your acts you attempt to free the slaves. You will not have them among you. You leave them where they are. Then what is to be the result? — I presume that local State governments will be preserved. If they are, if the people have a right to make their own laws, and to govern themselves, they will not only reënslave every person that you attempt to set free, but they will reënslave the whole race."

Nor has the horrid menace of reënslavement proceeded from the Senator from Delaware alone. It has been uttered even by Mr. Willey, the mild Senator from Virginia, speaking in the name of State Rights. Newspapers have taken up and repeated the revolting strain. That is to say, no matter what may be done for Emancipation, whether by Proclamation of the President, or by Congress even, the State, on resuming its place in the Union, will, in the exercise of its sovereign power, reënslave every colored person within its jurisdiction; and this is the menace from Delaware, and even from regenerated Western Virginia! I am obliged to Senators for their frankness. If I needed any additional motive for the urgency with which I assert the power of Congress, I should find it in the pretensions thus savagely proclaimed. In the name of Heaven, let us spare no effort to save the country from this shame, and an oppressed people from this additional outrage!

"Once free, always free." This is a rule of law, and an instinct of humanity. It is a self-evident axiom, which only tyrants and slave-traders have denied. The brutal pretension thus flamingly advanced, to reënslave those who have been set free, puts us all on our guard. There must be no chance or loop-hole for such an intolerable, Heaven-defying iniquity. Alas! there have been crimes in human history; but I know of none blacker than this. There have been acts of baseness; but I know of none more utterly vile. Against the possibility of such a sacrifice we must take a bond which cannot be set aside, — and this can be found only in the powers of Congress.

Congress has already done much. Besides its noble Act of Emancipation, it has provided that every person guilty of treason, or of inciting or assisting the Rebellion, "shall be disqualified to hold any office under the United States." And by another act, it has provided that every person elected or appointed to any office of honor or profit under the Government of the United States shall, before entering upon its duties, *take an oath* "that he has not voluntarily borne arms against the United States, or given aid, countenance, counsel, or encouragement to persons engaged in armed hostility thereto,

* Thirty-Seventh Congress, Second Session, 2d May, 1862, Part III. p. 1923.

www.ingramcontent.com/pod-product-compliance
Lightning Source LLC
LaVergne TN
LVHW020634110826
845149LV00004B/1176
9781418191429